Witness out of the Abyss

Jared James

BookLeaf Publishing
India | USA | UK

Presentation by *BookLeaf Publishing*

Web: www.bookleafpub.com

E-mail: info@bookleafpub.com

ISBN: 9789357211673

First edition 2023

DEDICATION

To all the ones who didn't survive and some of the ones that did.

ACKNOWLEDGEMENT

Thankyou God.
Thankyou to all survivors and believers, helpers and friends, and a special thank you to my parts who had the courage to speak up about the horrors they suffered after too many years in silence.

PREFACE

I WANT TO BE A PART OF THE GENERATION THAT STOPS HUMAN TRAFFICKING. DO YOU?

Qualifications?

Been through core splits
Been through child sexual abuse
Been through self harm
Been through suicide attempts
Been through alcohol addiction
Been through drug addiction
Been through satanic ritual abuse
Been through elite gender inversion
Been through electrocution
Been through blood rituals
Been through human sacrifice
Been through dissociative identity disorder
Been through poverty
Been through colour inversion
Been through homophobia
Been through transphobia
Been through racism
Been through illicit relationships
Been through paedophilic relationships
Been through grooming
Been through cPTSD
Been through gender identity disorder
Been through depression
Been through anxiety
Been through cannibalism
Been through necrophilia

Been through directed energy attacks (D. E. W)
Been through cloning
Been through stalking
Been through gang rape
Been through extreme torture
Been through branding
Been through incest
Been through child sexual abuse imagary
Been through coersive control
Been through paedophile rings
Been through human trafficking
Been through abusive relationships
Been through violence
Been through the death of my children
Been through my children being stolen
Been through kidnap
Been through murder
Been through voodoo
Been through black magic
Been through sadism
Been through degradation
Been through dehumanisation
Been through suicide programming
Been through mk ultra
Been through project monarch
Been through deep underground military bases
Been through the court system
Been through arrest and detention
Been through robbery

Been through catfishing
Been through hacking
Been through bribary
Been through identity theft
Been through fraud
Been through death threats
Been through madness
Lived through holy war
Survived through fucking hell.
What are your qualifications?

Fucked up Gratitude list

15 Nov. 01.14am

Smokes
Toilet roll
Avamys
Cat sleeps
Tea
Others survivors

Traffic

Sick of being trafficked,
Sick of being trafficked,
Sick of being trafficked,
Sick of being trafficked,
Sick of being trafficked,
Sick of being trafficked,
Sick of being trafficked,
Sick of being trafficked,
Sick of being trafficked,
Sick of being trafficked,
Sick of being trafficked,
Sick of being trafficked,
Sick of being trafficked,
FUCKING SICK of being trafficked,
Sickkk of beeeeiinnng trafficked,
Sick of being trafficked,
Guess what? I'm sick of being trafficked.
Sick of being trafficked-
-Sick of being TRAFFICKED.
Sick of BEING TRAFFICKED.
SICK OF BEING TRAFFICKED!!!

Done with:

Liars
Cheats
Incest
Black magic cunts
Voodoo
Thieves
Rapists
Paedophiles
Fake friends
Jealous family
Narcissists
Covens
Force

Shopping

Non alcohol peroni
Cat food soup
Cat treats
Baby oil
Multi vitamins
Kiwi
Gratefruit juice
Cat milk
Cucumber
Lemons
tonic
Pineapple

C. H. I. M. E

It don't rhyme
but It do chime
I done real time.
In a cult.

It don't rhyme
but It do chime
I done bad crimes.
In a cult.

It don't rhyme
but It do chime
covered in slime.
In a cult.

It don't rhyme
but It do chime
They hate sunshine.
In a cult.

It don't rhyme
but It do chime
Always night-time.
In a cult.

It don't rhyme
but It do chime
Stamp on heads to climb.
In a cult.

It don't rhyme
but it do chime
Bodies intertwine.
In a cult.

It don't rhyme
But It do chime
It's a human sign.
In a cult.

It don't rhyme
But It do chime
Nothing is fine.
In a cult.

It don't rhyme
But It do chime
A twisted paradigm.
In a cult.

It don't rhyme
But It do chime
A fucked up storyline.
From a cult.

The neon children

The neon children hate you.

The neon children hate you.

The neon children hate you.

Wow you really fucked up.

Mk-Ultra, D. I. D and memory loss.

Mk ultra d.i.d and memory loss,
Being a survivor of this type of trauma is difficult at best. New memories that were suppressed for years begin to surface. Sometimes this is through triggers and cues, buttons being pushed-purposely or accidental, othertimes just flashbacks uninvited arrive without any warning.

It takes more than a moment to adjust. Memories were buried deep, separated behind amnesia walls locked in by forced electrocution.

Many years may have passed since the incidents took place and yet after surfacing- they come alive again in real time- full HD with surround sound.

I have cptsd, insomnia, depression, anxiety & dissociative identity disorder.
This is my daily reality.
Some days I don't make it out of bed, others I'm cast backwards -trying to piece together

fragments of a life of suffering through child sexual abuse and mind control.

Im not exactly free of the life. I'm not fully up to date with all of my past.. The abuse is still fractured and doesn't always make sense until con-current pieces of memories are uncovered. I have big blocks of amnesia and missing time. Its draining.

Weaving together pieces of my uncovered past with the "day" memories I have of the times- seeing how it all fits together.
I have people trying to reprogram me. I still don't have a safe space away from perpetrators and the kind of power they want to extend over me.

To some I'm just another pawn in their game. Just another piece to collect. Just another way to stake a claim in something that is not their own. A narrative made of untruths and ruthless moves, regardless of the sacrifices it cost others to bare. A way up the greasy ladder. Stick a flag in it and call it yours. Shut me in another box and close the lid.

I didn't get to choose the life I was created into, I didn't get to choose what happened to me as an infant, as a child, as a teen. I didn't get to choose which parts to remember of the trauma I endured. It's not a game. And if it was---- it -----wouldn't----- be------ worth-------playing. It's not fun. I wouldn't recommend it.

Know this : It was EXTREME. So extreme my brain couldn't handle it. So extreme it re-wrote the neuron pathways in my brain. So extreme I dissociated from it for over 20 years before anything at all came back. Even then it was sparadic. It was hazy. It was fucking unbelievable if you want to know the truth. And I didn't want to believe it. I didn't want to be an mk-ultra test subject, or a child porn star. I didn't want to have d.i.d- and such bad shell shock that I can barely function day to day.

It's ruined my sense of self. Not only my childhood through the most traumatic abuse, but my now. This me.

I have to revisit the past often, the more supressed memories I learn about the harder it becomes. I have to rewrite my history to include this "new" truth. These new memories shift everything and nothing of my childhood is left untouched.

Then comes the grief. A grief for the loss of my dissociative front life which has now been obliterated by the horrifying reality. Almost everything I believed has been a l-i-e. A construct. A test. And I don't trust the testers.

Mind control.
Abuse.
Handlers.
Abuse.
Strangers.
Abuse.
Relatives.
Abuse.
Abuse. Abuse. Abuse.

It's rocked my foundations.
I'm in a storm, stood in the rubble surrounded by the swirling debris. Covered in dust.

Forget
Forget
Forget.
ZAP. ZAP. ZAP.

Forget.

ZAP.

Forget.

ZAP.

....

F

.

o

.

r

.

g

.

e

.

t

...

.

.

ZAP

.

.

.

.

.

Mk ultra d.i.d and memory loss

Being a survivor of this type of trauma is difficult at best. New memories that were suppressed for years begin to surface. Sometimes this is through triggers and cues, buttons being pushed-purposely or accidental, othertimes just flashbacks uninvited arrive without any warning.

It takes more than a moment to adjust. Memories were buried deep, separated behind amnesia walls locked in by forced electrocution.

Many years may have passed since the incidents took place and yet after surfacing- they come alive again in real time- full HD with surround sound.

I have cptsd, insomnia, depression, anxiety & dissociative identity disorder.
This is my daily reality.
Some days I don't make it out of bed, others I'm cast backwards -trying to piece together fragments of a life of suffering through child sexual abuse and mind control.

Im not exactly free of the life. I'm not fully up to date with all of my past.. The abuse is still fractured and doesn't always make sense until con-current pieces of memories are uncovered. I have big blocks of amnesia and missing time. Its draining.

Weaving together pieces of my uncovered past with the "day" memories I have of the times- seeing how it all fits together.
I have people trying to reprogram me. I still don't have a safe space away from perpetrators

and the kind of power they want to extend over me.

To some I'm just another pawn in their chess game. Just another piece to collect. Just another way to stake a claim in something that is not their own. A narrative made of untruths and ruthless moves, regardless of the sacrifices it cost others to bare. A way up the greasy ladder. Stick a flag in it and call it yours. Shut me in another box and close the lid.

I didn't get to choose the life I was created into, I didn't get to choose what happened to me as an infant, as a child, as a teen. I didn't get to choose which parts to remember of the trauma I endured. It's not a game. And if it was---- it -----wouldn't----- be------ worth-------playing. It's not fun. I wouldn't recommend it.

Know this : It was EXTREME. So extreme my brain couldn't handle it. So extreme it re-wrote the neuron pathways in my brain. So extreme I dissociated from it for over 20 years before anything at all came back. Even then it was sparadic. It was hazy. It was fucking unbelievable if you want to know the truth. And I didn't want to believe it. I didn't want to be an mk-ultra test subject, or a child porn star. I didn't want to have d.i.d- and such bad shell shock that I can barely function day to day.

It's ruined my sense of self. Not only my childhood through the most traumatic abuse, but my now. This me.
I have to revisit the past often, the more supressed memories I learn about the harder it becomes. I have to rewrite my history to include this "new" truth. These new memories shift everything and nothing of my childhood is left untouched.

Then comes the grief. A grief for the loss of my dissociative front life which has now been obliterated by the horrifying reality. Almost everything I believed has been a l-i-e. A construct. A test. And I don't trust the testers.

Mind control.
Abuse.
Handlers.
Abuse.
Strangers.
Abuse.
Relatives.
Abuse.
Abuse. Abuse. Abuse.

It's rocked my foundations.
I'm in a storm, stood in the rubble surrounded by the swirling debris. Covered in dust.

Forget
Forget
Forget.
ZAP. ZAP. ZAP.

Forget.

ZAP.

Forget.

ZAP.
....
F
.
o
.
r
.
g

.

e

.

t

...

.

.

ZAP

.

.

.

Mk ultra d.i.d and memory loss

Being a survivor of this type of trauma is difficult at best. New memories that were suppressed for years begin to surface. Sometimes this is through triggers and cues, buttons being pushed-purposely or accidental, othertimes just flashbacks uninvited arrive without any warning.

It takes more than a moment to adjust. Memories were buried deep, separated behind amnesia walls locked in by forced electrocution.

Many years may have passed since the incidents took place and yet after surfacing- they come alive again in real time- full HD with surround sound.

I have cptsd, insomnia, depression, anxiety & dissociative identity disorder.
This is my daily reality.
Some days I don't make it out of bed, others I'm cast backwards -trying to piece together fragments of a life of suffering through child sexual abuse and mind control.

Im not exactly free of the life. I'm not fully up to date with all of my past.. The abuse is still fractured and doesn't always make sense until con-current pieces of memories are uncovered. I have big blocks of amnesia and missing time. Its draining.

Weaving together pieces of my uncovered past with the "day" memories I have of the times- seeing how it all fits together.
I have people trying to reprogram me. I still don't have a safe space away from perpetrators and the kind of power they want to extend over me.

To some I'm just another pawn in their chess game. Just another piece to collect. Just another way to stake a claim in something that is not their own. A narrative made of untruths and ruthless moves, regardless of the sacrifices it cost others to bare. A way up the greasy ladder. Stick a flag in it and call it yours. Shut me in another box and close the lid.

I didn't get to choose the life I was created into, I didn't get to choose what happened to me as an infant, as a child, as a teen. I didn't get to choose which parts to remember of the trauma I endured. It's not a game. And if it was---- it -----wouldn't----- be------ worth-------playing. It's not fun. I wouldn't recommend it.

Know this : It was EXTREME. So extreme my brain couldn't handle it. So extreme it re-wrote the neuron pathways in my brain. So extreme I dissociated from it for over 20 years before anything at all came back. Even then it was sparadic. It was hazy. It was fucking unbelievable if you want to know the truth. And I didn't want to believe it. I didn't want to be an mk-ultra test subject, or a child porn star. I didn't want to have d.i.d- and such bad shell shock that I can barely function day to day.

It's ruined my sense of self. Not only my childhood through the most traumatic abuse, but my now. This me.

I have to revisit the past often, the more supressed memories I learn about the harder it becomes. I have to rewrite my history to include this "new" truth. These new memories shift everything and nothing of my childhood is left untouched.

It's rocked my foundations.

I'm in a storm, stood in the rubble surrounded by the swirling debris. Covered in dust.

Then comes the grief. A grief for the loss of my dissociative front life which has now been obliterated by the horrifying reality. Almost everything I believed has been a l-i-e. A construct. A test. And I don't trust the testers.

Mind control.
Abuse.
Handlers.
Abuse.
Strangers.
Abuse.
Relatives.
Abuse.
Abuse. Abuse. Abuse.

It's rocked my foundations.
I'm in a storm, stood in the rubble surrounded by the swirling debris. Covered in dust.

Forget
Forget
Forget.
ZAP. ZAP. ZAP.

Forget.

ZAP.

Forget.

ZAP.

....

F

.

o

.

r

.

g

.

e

.

t

...

.

.

ZAP

.

.

Where was I?

Oh yes the trust. Or the lack of it.
I don't trust. Not anyone. Not anymore.
I did.
Before.
I was made to regret
it.
Over
and
over
again.

It's an unfortunate side effect of my current reality. I just cannot trust people. Sometimes I can't even trust myself- me being a programmed multiple and all. Not all my parts are on script. I still have some inner work to do here.

And so this is my reality. This is where I'm at. Going to go look at cute pictures of animals now. I'm done having my head shrunk for the time being.

.

.

.

Mk ultra d.i.d and memory loss

Being a survivor of this type of trauma is difficult at best. New memories that were suppressed for years begin to surface. Sometimes this is through triggers and cues, buttons being pushed-purposely or accidental, othertimes just flashbacks uninvited arrive without any warning.

It takes more than a moment to adjust. Memories were buried deep, separated behind amnesia walls locked in by forced electrocution.

Many years may have passed since the incidents took place and yet after surfacing- they come alive again in real time- full HD with surround sound.

I have cptsd, insomnia, depression, anxiety & dissociative identity disorder.
This is my daily reality.
Some days I don't make it out of bed, others I'm cast backwards -trying to piece together fragments of a life of suffering through child sexual abuse and mind control.

Im not exactly free of the life. I'm not fully up to date with all of my past.. The abuse is still fractured and doesn't always make sense until con-current pieces of memories are uncovered. I have big blocks of amnesia and missing time. Its draining.

Weaving together pieces of my uncovered past with the "day" memories I have of the times- seeing how it all fits together.
I have people trying to reprogram me. I still don't have a safe space away from perpetrators and the kind of power they want to extend over me.

To some I'm just another pawn in their chess game. Just another piece to collect. Just another way to stake a claim in something that is not their own. A narrative made of untruths and ruthless moves, regardless of the sacrifices it cost others to bare. A way up the greasy ladder. Stick a flag in it and call it yours. Shut me in another box and close the lid.

I didn't get to choose the life I was created into, I didn't get to choose what happened to me as an infant, as a child, as a teen. I didn't get to choose which parts to remember of the trauma I endured. It's not a game. And if it was---- it

-----wouldn't----- be------ worth-------playing. It's not fun. I wouldn't recommend it.

Know this : It was EXTREME. So extreme my brain couldn't handle it. So extreme it re-wrote the neuron pathways in my brain. So extreme I dissociated from it for over 20 years before anything at all came back. Even then it was sparadic. It was hazy. It was fucking unbelievable if you want to know the truth. And I didn't want to believe it. I didn't want to be an mk-ultra test subject, or a child porn star. I didn't want to have d.i.d- and such bad shell shock that I can barely function day to day.

It's ruined my sense of self. Not only my childhood through the most traumatic abuse, but my now. This me.
I have to revisit the past often, the more supressed memories I learn about the harder it becomes. I have to rewrite my history to include this "new" truth. These new memories shift everything and nothing of my childhood is left untouched.

It's rocked my foundations.
I'm in a storm, stood in the rubble surrounded by the swirling debris. Covered in dust.

Then comes the grief. A grief for the loss of my dissociative front life which has now been obliterated by the horrifying reality. Almost everything I believed has been a l-i-e. A construct. A test. And I don't trust the testers.

Mind control.
Abuse.
Handlers.
Abuse.
Strangers.
Abuse.
Relatives.
Abuse.
Abuse. Abuse. Abuse.

It's rocked my foundations.
I'm in a storm, stood in the rubble surrounded by the swirling debris. Covered in dust.

Forget
Forget
Forget.
ZAP. ZAP. ZAP.

Forget.

ZAP.

Forget.

ZAP.

....

F

.

o

.

r

.

g

.

e

.

t

...

.

.

ZAP

.

.

Where was I?

.

.

.

Fetus 1

Sacrifices to Moloch/Baal/Lucifer.
Abortion is a emotive topic right now. The recent discussions around the ethics of full term abortion and planned parenthood selling fetuses. The black market in fetuses is a issue that many are not aware of.

Also the use of fetal tissues in vaccines and "beauty products" is worth researching considering the links between satanic ritual abuse and big pharma.
As a survivor of SRA I have witnessed and been part of some of the fetus and infant ritual offerings to these "gods".

In utero and first born children are sometimes sacrificed for the cult. This is a offering that is presented to solidify cult bonds and loyalties.
I have seen fetuses liquidised in a blender and used in rituals (drinking or lathering on skin to evoke demons) .

I have seen babies skinned alive and then used as live sacrifices. Babies discarded after torture in such ways left in the neighbourhood bins, skips etc. Used to emotionally blackmail the cult member (parent- usually mother) or as a punishment for perceived disloyalty/disobedience - humiliation rituals.

These are our Children.

These are our Babies.

These are our Fetuses.

Wombs are harvested by breeders for the cult. Certain cult members are used as breeders as a main purpose. Breeding child sex slaves or others depending on cult rank and station.

A group of men had sex with xxxx child then ejaculated in the same glass and this liquid was then inserted into the "breeder". The "winning" sperm fertilised the woman and the baby was subsequently aborted to seal a particular request from the "gods".

Requests and uses can vary. Satanic calenders lists the major dates for human sacrifice but fetuses and babies can be sacrificed on other days depending on the circumstances.
Most people think the times of human sacrifice is over. Think again. It is happening on a world wide scale every night of the week. This is cult business. This is the real Apocalypto. The Mel Gibson film brought to life in full gory detail. It is vile. It is horrific. It needs to stop.

Small rectangle of HOPE

Inside this small dank cell deep underground.
Steady water slowly drips.
A heavy door slammed shut. Now isolated in the ice cold room. Darkness envelops the space.
Breath of white smokes in the dark. Eyes adjust.
A small rectangle of light from the corridor beyond- A far off horizon, glistens in the shadow of the locked door.
Senses depressed. Nothingness. The void. The abyss. The darkness.
Silence.
A small child in the centre of the room curled fetal trying to stay warm. Tiny hairs all over the body stand up straight on mottled skin.
Knees tucked under chin. Arms wrapped around themselves, draw the legs up closer. A tiny ball. Insignificant.
Cheek touching the icy stone slab of the cell floor. A searing pain turns to numbness in the minutes that turn slowly into hours. Drip drip drip the only sound.
One two three four.
Shivers. Rubbing blue numbed hands over pursed skin.
A decision.

A choice to make.
To piss or not to piss? Heat or no heat? Temporary comfort and relief. A welcomed distraction.
Unknown quantities. Trying to gauge a correct decision with too many variables beyond control. How much longer can be endured in this cell? This deprivation. Is it worth a tempory pool of warmth? It depends.
Too many times no one comes. The realisation that it is always a gamble. Timing critical. Never knowing how much longer the isolation will be. No certainties of anything apart from the steady ache of torture. The piss invariably turns cold. And now teeth chatter, bite down on gums, frozen shivers jolt up the spine.
Hands squeezed together clasping. Eyes shut tight. Prayer to God. Recite the hymns from school assembly. Forget the words can only hum the tune. So fucking cold. So cold. So cold. Involuntary shivers turn to full body spasms. Focus to control.
A distant noise drawers closer. A one two like the beat of a drum keeps time to the hymn.
One.
Two.
One two.
One.
Two.

One- Two dark shapes form in the slivered horizon.

The light outline of shiny ink black boots at the door. A slim rectangle of hope.

A key in the lock loudly turns.

The heavy door creaks open. Golden light floods into the monochrome dank cell. Suddenly prayers answered.

Slowly lifting numb cheek up from stone.

Shaking hands press down into the wetness of the icy pool. Pushes up. Tries to stand. Frozen shivers jolt up the spine.

Home time.

The Grateful WED

7 Sept. 01.55am

Books
Mumbai chicken
Zero alcohol Red wine
Menthol cigarettes
Moving house
A friend
Dark nights
The sound of trees
Salt bath
Tears
Lists
Poems

Beat me, hate me

A young black boy all dressed in tan,
bellbottoms or flared trousers. With bigger boys
all dressed the same, afro hair, very neat looking.

A small room, looks like a dressing room.

The smallest boy remains.

Stripped naked.

Bent over a table.
Getting buggered by some old violent men.
Angry aggressive types. Revellers.
They shout insults at him, call him ugly. "Big
nxxxer nose."
Punch him in the face whilst raping him.
"why you so ugly boy?"
"you's ugly"
"you cxxn. Fuckin' cxxn. Fuckin' nxxxer. Sing
nxxxer sing, dance for us"
They jeering and laughing. Tears stream down
his face. They line up and take turns to rape him.
They beat on him and call him a dog. They spit
in his face.

I see a man. Smart dress, 50s style, fedora and spats.
Pinstripes and cigar smoke. Big jewelry, rings on fingers.
Smokes his cigar, watches on.
His fat hands count money.
Pointed beedy eyes dart around the room.
Cigar smoke and pinstripes.

Journal 2.05am

Drained. Tired. Bored. Sick of this shit.
LIES
Lies
Lies
Lies
Lies
Lies
Boundaries.

So I am still awake. Tired of playing games
with people who show no regard for my feelings
or respect for my free will decisions.
What constitutes family?

What's most important?

I decide to place peace over drama.

I decide to choose solitude over disrespect.

I know my worth.
I know my truth.

I'm not willing to be manipulated anymore.

So it gets empty. It gets lonely. But it's better than the alternative.
I can't go back. I can't go back to that so called life. I can't give up my reality for the insanity of the lies and bullshit of those unwilling to heal.

I must respect myself enough to walk away and start again.

It didn't have to be like this. But I can't choose for them. And I can't go back to incestuous tethering. NOT FOR ANYONE.

I believe in freedom.
I believe in a world without sexual slavery being sold as family loyalty.
I want to be free. Free to choose for myself.
I DESERVE a life of my own. Its been xx years of hell
That's slavery and I'm done.
Freedom beckons.
I heed the call 🕊

Metal cages. 1.0

Rows and rows of metal cages.
Like a hallway on either side.

I'm in one and I see other naked children
opposite and at either side.

Sometimes they come and pluck children out
and take them away for testing.

You can hear screaming and sometimes you can
recognise the child.

I make friends with my eyes with some children.
We have a little conversation without saying
anything.
We are not allowed to talk to each other.
Sometimes they come back with cake.
And what they had to do to get it is

Worse

Than

Death.

I eat scabs and my finger nails.

I never choose one that I prefer.

I make notes in my mind of who likes what cakes.

And I feed other children, but in secret- as we are not supposed to interact unless we are torturing each other in a test.

Gratitude shit

Feeling my feelings - specially the knarly ones
that I'm no longer ashamed of.
Honesty
Bed
Duvet
Tonic water
Ancestors
Clarity
Chorus
Old earth peoples
Steel drums
Cigarettes
Suicidal thoughts
Sleep

Anxious Things.

I cannot control everything
I can only control myself.
Being scared is natural
It is transitional.
I don't understand what is happening.
I am scared.
I feel disgusting.
I feel creeped.
It feels like whatever I do it is the wrong thing.
I have stomach ache.
I woke up I want the pain to stop.
I don't know how to stop the pain.
I feel sexually violated.
I want to leave. But I don't know where to go.
I can hear noise but it doesn't make sense to me.
I feel threatened.
It is scaring me.
I feel like a tiny child.
I need help but I don't know how to get the help
I need.
I feel lost.

GRITitude Tuesday

Smokes.
Chocolate.
Sea.
Mashed potato.
Khalid.
T.A
Washing machine.
Alcohol free beer.
No longer being drunk to cope with emotional disregulation.
Noise cancelling headphones.
Not being that A hole.
Socks.
Homeless people helping me out.
Refugee kitchens.

Manifest

Honesty

Integrity

Values

Real connections

Vibes

Peace

Love

Fucked up gratitude 4.02am

Cigarettes.
Tonic.
Phone.
Rain noise.
Shorts.
Cat.
Boundaries- even if they are ignored.
Baby on the bus.
Sunglasses. Crying.
Banana. Sandwich. Tea.
Bed.
Wind. Cool breeze.
Shoes.
Socks.
Jeans.
Lists.
Sleep.

Metal cages 2.0

I'm still in the bunker. Many children are picked out of metal cages. Taken to a classroom.
They tell us we are dogs and most of the children really start to believe it.

They feed you on the floor, they tell you it's better to be a dog than a girl.
Knowing what they do to girls you start to wish that you was
a dog.
To be a good dog you have to be obedient. The train you up in ways I can't remember.

In the classroom we all have separate desks. We are wired up to electric shock treatment.
We each have a button to press of electricity.
If you press it electrocutes another child.
If you keep pressing you do well and get electrocuted less.

Most of the children are pressing their button frantic. The electric shocks hurt alot.
I think the are inside of us.
In our vaginas or arses or both.

I refuse to press.
I'm not playing. Pretty soon I pass out from all the electricity.
I dont get to eat today.
I'm back in the freezer on my own.

D. U. M. B

I'm in a drawer naked. They wheel you under something like I'm in a tray. They keep checking up to see if I'll agree to do sex things with some old men.
I refuse and back under I go. Naked with no room to move. Its dark and I can hear metallic noises. I'm in a bunker deep underground. They are wearing lab coats.
The noise travels in a weird way down here underground. Many times they come to see og the little sex princess will come out to play.
I say inside.
I refuse.
This goes on for a very long time.

Eventually I say yes she will come out.
They make me get showered. I properly smell.
I'm covered in my own piss and shit.
I haven't eaten in what feels like days.
I ate some snot and drank some tears while I was inside the drawer.
The drawer becomes a a trigger to dissociate.
At some point a relative comes to coerce me and I get a warm cup of baby blood to drink.
It smells really bad and it sticks to my teeth.

The fact that it's warm is the worst part.
It makes me vibrate at a different level.
And then I have to have sex with someone who liked to hurt me.
This is how they make you do porn.

www.ingramcontent.com/pod-product-compliance
Lightning Source LLC
Chambersburg PA
CBHW051736130826
49812CB00033B/884